Alberto De Luigi

Critical Review of Gerring and Thacker's Centripetal Theory of Democratic Governance

createspace[tm]

ISBN-13: 978-1512278750
ISBN-10: 1512278750

Printed by CreateSpace
Charleston (SC)
May 2015

Table of contents

Introduction

In this essay it is proposed a critical analysis of Gerring and Thacker's centripetal theory of democratic governance, referring to their work published in 2008. At first a brief summary of the theory will be provided, showing the ambiguities concerning the association between the name of the theory – "Centripetalism", according to the authors a mix of authority and inclusion – and its substantial and practical contents. Then will be debated Gerring and Thacker's claim to have conceived a "refinement of Lijphart's consensus model" (or "a fundamental reconceptualization" of it) [p.190, 2008]. In fact will be explained in detail why any parallelism between centripetal theory and power sharing model is completely inconsistent, since the centripetal theory is actually incompatible with Lijphart's model and, in many respects, the opposite. At the end, will be discussed a critic of Gerring and Thacker's methodology for what concerns causal mechanisms and aggregation of variables at the basis of the empirical verification of the theory, showing why their centripetal theory of democratic governance can be considered too far-reaching (but even too less characterized by its own peculiar traits!) to have a real explanatory power.

1.   Centripetalism

In order to explain the concept of Centripetalism Gerring and Thacker provide both a theoretical and practical definition. In theory, Centripetalism is a mix of inclusion and authority: "the first indicates the extent to which political institutions are designed to incorporate a diversity of interests, ideas, and identities in the process of governance", the second "the extent to which political institutions centralize constitutional sovereignty within a democratic framework" [p. 16, 2008]. Furthermore, the authors underline the fact that "Centripetalism is rightly regarded as a modification of the British Westminster model along Continental lines" and precisely it consists in the "intellectual lineage of Centralism along with the criticisms leveled by advocates of PR" [p. 15]. The Westiminster model is characterised by strong unitary government, strong parties, flexible constitution, and first-past-the-post elections with two party dominance. Since the modification along Continental lines introduces PR system instead of first-past-the-post, then majoritarian elections and the two-party dominance, peculiar features of Centralism, are not considered features of Centripetalism. In fact the authors seem to perceive as alarming a system of "centralized powers in the hands of two political parties" [p. 13]. Nevertheless, it's not immediate to imagine what is the peculiar organizational form of Centripetalism that produces strong governments and strong parties, if those "centralist" features of the British model are excluded. For what regards strong governments, the authors' answer would be Unitarism, that is conducive to less competition (or less conflicts) between central government and other federal institutions. In their view, this would produce better governance. On the other side, the peculiar feature strengthening parties is the closed list electoral system, promoting inter-party competition rather than intra-party [p. 34-35]: this increases unity inside the party and thus accountability and good government, while dissidents within a party can choose to "exit" and form other parties (thanks to a low threshold in PR system) if "voice" mechanisms fail.

Apparently, at this point the only features taken from the Westminster model, exemplificative of Centralism, are Unitarism (instead of Federalism) and flexible constitutions. The discussion of the last relies on Walter Bagehot's work, *The English Constitution*, where is discussed how the splitting of sovereignty into many parts amount to no sovereignty: thus is better to choose simple constitutions where the ultimate power relies upon a single authority.

To sum up, the "practical" organizational forms suggested by the theory of Centripetalism, that according to the authors are "modelled on the Continental European polity" [p. 16], are the following: Unitarism rather than Federalism; Parliamentarism rather than presidentialism; closed list proportional system, rather than single-member district and majoritarianism; congruent elections; few elective offices; strong parties;

multiparty competition rather than two-party; popular referenda only at the instigation of the legislature (or not at all). According to these features, the authors state that Scandinavian countries offer the best example of Centripetalism, while United States stand at the opposite. But at this point it seems that remains few of the original Westminster "centralist" paradigm in favour of a switch towards other models (that the authors themselves refers to as "Continental European polity").

2.   Comparisons with Lijphart's Consensus Model

As first thing, we should note that this conception of Centripetalism is quite different from the previous literature, and is not always clear how and which ones of its practical features rely on the two theoretical paradigms underlying the theory: authority and inclusion. According to Lijphart, Centripetalism refers to homogeneus and stable democracies [p. 36, 2007], and he uses the term referring specifically to the Anglo-American democracies, even if he associates also Scandinavian countries to this category [p. 28] (in this way resembling closer the position of Gerring and Thacker). But Lijphart's theoretical context is very different, since he uses the concept of centripetal countries in contrast with fragmented and unstable democracies (the Continental European, or centrifugal democracies), and this framework is the basis for his theory of consociational or consensus democracies, which are deviant cases of fragmented and stable countries. Furthermore, he associates to this theoretical framework organizational and political forms that are at odds with what proposed by Gerring and Thacker's centripetal theory. The fact that the two authors ask themselves whether their work is best viewed as a "refinement of Lijphart's consensus model", or as a "fundamental reconceptualization" of it[1], is particularly curious, since any association between the two theories seems far-fetched. It's clear that they do not refer to "fragmented" democracies when dealing with their theory, they neither seem to face the issue of fragmentation as conducive to instability. They work around the problem, listing what are the organizational forms that can be conducive to fragmentation and therefore what shall be avoided[2]. Instead, the purpose of Lijphart is to show what are the organizational forms[3] that can better deal with a fragmentation "already in place". He has a completely different perspective, and it may even depend on the fact that Gerring and Thacker's work is based on long-run considerations, where institutions produce social and

---

[1] "The question of whether the present work is best viewed as a refinement of Lijphart's consensus model, or as a fundamental reconceptualization, need not detain us. We would be delighted with either formulation" (Gerring and Thacker [p. 190, 2008])

[2] For instance, Gerring and Thacker explains that the structure of Federalism has generated the separation of federal and provincial party system, and for this reason it is a recipe for disjointed federal/territorial politics (Gerring and Thacker [p. 42-43, 2008])

[3] The organizational forms he highlights are actually the features of consociational democracies

environmental consequences (new institutionalism[4]), rather than being a short-run remedy to pre-existent and exogenously given conditions, as it seem to pertain more to Lijphart theory (but this doesn't mean that they do exclude completely considerations of the other type).

Gerring and Thacker, reviewing Lijphart's power sharing theory, list the elements of his theory in two distinct dimensions: an *executive-parties* dimension and a *federal-unity* dimension. The first dimension comprises five variables that according to the authors "closely resembles the centripetal model" (Gerring and Thacker [p. 189, 2008]): 1) a multiparty system, 2) broad multiparty coalitions, 3) executive-legislative balance of power, 4) proportional representation, 5) coordinated, "corporatist" interest group systems aimed at compromise and concertation. Surprisingly, the authors reject the whole *federal-unity* dimension without discussing the reasons Lijphart argues for that. They simply state that "only the first dimension shows a consistent relationship to good governance across Lijphart's chosen sample of thirty-six long-term democracies" [p. 189, 2008]. Thus, Centripetalism reject the following forms adopted by Lijphart's consensus model: 6) federal and decentralized government, 7) Bicameralism with two equally strong but different houses, 8) rigid constitutions 9) systems in which laws are subject to judicial review, 10) independent central banks.

---

[4] For example Gerring and Thacker say that "institutions also condition the creation and reproduction of interests and identities [p. 19, 2008]

The motivation to the adoption of the five variables of the first dimension as elements of Centripetalism is not completely clear: in fact we don't even see immediate connection between all of these variables and the theoretical basis underlying Centripetalism[5]. It is a theory, according to what summarized above, inspired to some elements of Centralism (Westminster model) – while other elements are rejected in favour of Continental European elements – plus the combination of authority and inclusion. Stated in this way it appears a bit ambiguous, and actually it is. Many examples can be provided. First, broad multiparty coalitions seem to be an inclusive feature, but this can be at odds with the authority principle. The same can be said about collegial cabinets (favoured by both consensus and centripetal model), and the executive-legislative balance of power. To balance different powers is inspired to the value of inclusion, but may conflict with the principle of authority, which would resemble more the executive dominance. On the other way round, there are features that embody the principle of authority and at the same time deny manifestly the principle of inclusion, for example "popular referenda only at instigation of the legislature" (or no popular referenda at all). Finally, it's not clear why Centripetalism should reject any kind of judicial review

---

[5] The fact that these variables are statistically consistent with good governance is not a pertinent motivation: the fact of being conducive to good governance is the reason why we should choose these variables (it has a normative implication), not the reason why the particular theory of Centripetalism, with its own features and theoretical basis, should incorporate these variables.

to legislation and why should oppose the independence of central bank, while on the other hand it accepts a balance between legislative and executive. An answer may be that the majority rule (which we assume determines the outcome of legislative and executive processes, not the sentences of a Supreme Court), is supposed to be superior to the other institutions present in a system of check and balances. This answer can be consistent with the demand for authority, but again, it's likely to undermine minority rights and, in the end, inclusion.

If the combination of inclusion and authority doesn't suggest satisfactory explanations, even the original roots in the British model cannot help Centripetalism to reach a proper soundness. In fact, none of the *executive-parties* variables listed above belongs to the Westminster model; rather, they're at the opposite. But since they seem to be elements at the very core of a political theory and they're not certainly negligible, then it's not clear why to insist in maintaining a link with the centralist model. Only the features of rigid constitutions, Unitarism and strong parties may constitute a connection, being common elements of Centralism and Centripetalism. Nevertheless, these three features can be merely coincidental, while if there is some connection among them it is not clarified by the authors. If even there was a connection of these variables in the Westminster model, it would hardly seem that in a totally different context (the centripetal model, that shall be featured by all the five *execetuive-parties* variables listed above) these three centralist variables can exhibit themselves linked together precisely because of the same patterns and connections exhibited in the Westminster model, and not because of coincidental reasons! For example, in Centripetalism, parties are supposed to be strong because of closed list PR system, not because of other features of the British model, not shared by the centripetal one (like for example the majoritarian system with two party dominance). Strong parties are, in this case, a common feature of the two models only because of coincidental reasons (or in any case because of reasons that are not clarified).

The ambiguity of Gerring and Thacker's centripetal theory come to light especially when we try to imagine whether a feature the authors didn't expressly deal with is included or not in their theory. For example, elements of consensus democracies are autonomous schools and minority rights (and in general, cultural autonomy) (Lijphart [p.46, 2007]); what about Centripetalism? To foster religious or linguistic policies is usually associates to federal institutions, or anyway, in long term it can produce social thrusts towards Federalism. Instead if the opposite policies are implemented (more authority, less autonomy), inclusion can be denied, especially in particular contexts of non-homogenous (fragmented) societies. In this case the two principles, inclusion and authority, are even more conflicting, and the practical organizational forms Gerring and Thacker propose seem completely arbitrary and dissociated with the theoretical framework of their theory.

When the two authors deal with the philosophical framework of Centripetalism, instead of discussing the political and electoral forms that it suggests, they show yet another view of their theory. In this perspective, Centripetalism seems a normative theory ascribable to the strand of thought of communitarian political philosophy more than an object of study of comparative politics:

> *"Centripetal institutions gather broadly; their roots are deep, that is, embedded. Through these institutions diverse interests, ideas, and identities ("interests," for short) are aggregated. Particularistic interests are converted into ideologies; ideologies are converted into general-interest appeals; parochial perspectives are nationalized. Centripetal institutions thus encourage a search for common ground. Centripetal institutions should culminate in an authoritative decision-making process, one not easily waylaid by minority objections. Institutions pull toward the center, offering incentives to participate and disincentives to defect"*
>
> Gerring and Thacker [p. 20, 2008]

Moreover, if the centralist paradigm (more authority, less inclusion) can be associated with tyranny and authoritarianism[6], Centripetalism (more authority, more inclusion) even seems to work fine in totalitarian frameworks. Reading in this perspective the abstract above taken from Gerring and Thacker, the parallelism between their conception of Centripetalism and Totalitarianism seems so strict to be almost alarming. We should

---

[6] Even if not explicit, it seems a concern of Gerring and Thacker, who write: "centralized power in the hands of two political parties and – more alarmingly, perhaps – in the hands of the person who happened to lead the majority party". [p. 13, 2008].

note that only closed list PR, Unitarism and Parliamentarism are the variables included in the empirical testing of the theory: this means that great part of centripetal theory relies only on theoretical hypotheses with a strong normative purpose, rather than merely being a description of causal mechanisms linking good governance and organizational forms and showing them as statistically consistent. Acknowledging this last point, it appears even a bit unfair to reject some variables included in the *federal-unity* dimension and favoured by Lijphart – without discussing the reasons he argues in support of them – stating simply that the only *executive-parties* dimension shows a consistent relationship to good governance in the sample he used. In fact not even Gerring and Thacker seem to have provided an empirical test about many variables they include as features of their theory: among them, flexible constitutions, systems in which laws are not subject to judicial review and central banks dependent from the government[7].

Finally, the list of what is incompatible between consociational democracies and Centripetalism is too broad (and variables involved are too important) to state that Centripetalism can be seen as a refinement (or a reconceptualization) of Lijphart's model. Power sharing theory is incompatible or even antithetical to centripetal theory for many reasons. First, the five key features listed above are the opposite of centripetal variables: Federalism, Bicameralism, rigid constitutions, judicial review and

---

[7] corresponding to the opposites of the consensus democracy features 8, 9 and 10 in the list above

independent central banks. In this respect, practical examples are extremely clear: Gerring and Thacker list 116 democracies ordered according to the degree of Centripetalism. In the list, best cases of centripetal democracy are Denmark, Sweden, Iceland and Norway (Gerring and Thacker [p. 98, 2008]), while Switzerland and India, that are two good (if not the best) examples of Lijphart's consensus democracies, are only mid-list or in the second half (they are ranked respectively number 49 and 61 out of 116). A second reason for incompatibility between the two views is the fact that power sharing theory has its purpose in making fragmented democracies more stable, while Centripetalism is aimed to provide a general theory of good governance; thus they have two very different target. Third, there are many other elements of consociational democracies that we can infer are in contrast with centripetal tendencies, though not expressely dealt by Gerring and Thacker's analysis. One of them, for instance, is the support to minority vetoes, minority rights and in general cultural and institutional autonomies (Lijphart [p. 43, 2007]), while on the contrary, as already quoted: "Centripetal institutions should culminate in an authoritative decision-making process, one not easily waylaid by minority objections". Another one is the promotion of broad representation, not only in cabinets and parliaments, but also in the civil service, judiciary, police and military (Lijphart [p. 84, 2007]), even instituting quotas for minorities (though not rigid quotas)[p. 71-74, 2007]; this is in conflict with either Gerring and Thacker's preference for "few elective offices" [p. 16, 2007] and their discussion against Lebanese electoral system of ethnic quotas (Gerring and Thacker [p. 58, 2008]), stemming from Horowitz's analysis (Horowitz, [p. 633, 1985]).

The fact that closed list PR electoral system and Parliamentarism are common to both the theories is not sufficient to justify a significant connection. Moreover, the fact that this two common features represent two variables, out of three, used by Gerring and Thacker empirical testing, suggests how little their theory (or at least what is empirically tested) is characterized by its own peculiar traits. Actually the three variables used for empirical analysis are merely Unitarism, closed list PR and Parliamentarism. The fact of choosing only these variables leaves unexplored and untested many specific correlations and causal mechanism included in Gerring and Thacker's theory, then it weakens the correspondence between theory (far more broad) and what is tested (few variables). The fact that these traits (apart from Unitarism) are not even intuitively connected with the term "Centripetalism" (why Parliamentarism and proportional system should be labelled as centripetal features?), only contributes to worsen the soundness and the explanatory power of Gerring and Thacker centripetal theory.

Finally, the two authors seem to assume credits they don't deserve when they raise critics to Lijphart: "Lijphart ignores or downplay certain additional causal mechanisms that we believe to be central to the achievement of good governance, for example, strong political parties" [p. 189, 2008]. Conversely, a year before the publication of Gerring and Thacker's essay,

Lijphart stated that "PR with closed lists can encourage the formation and maintenance of strong and cohesive political parties" [p. 79, 2007]. He defined in advance what is exactly the causal relationship determined by Gerring and Thacker between closed list and strong political parties, that is, incidentally, the reason why they chose this electoral form as a part of their centripetal theory. Clearly they are not updated (thus neither innovative), since last Lijphart's work appearing among their references is *Patterns of Democracy* (1999).

3.   **Empirics**

The empirical part of Gerring and Thacker's essay attracts skepticism and criticism on several counts, as marked by Timothy Hellwig in his review (2009)[8] of *A Centripetal Theory of Democratic Governance.* The author calls into question if Centripetalism is adequately represented by three indicators and asks why, "after convincingly arguing its importance in the causal story, is party government not included in the empirical tests" (Hellwig [p. 1000-1001, 2009]). In the paragraph above these criticisms are analysed more in depth, but there are other

---

[8] "In the course of their analysis, Gerring and Thacker make several choices that invite skepticism" (Hellwig [p. 1000, 2009])

doubts raised by Hellwig, as well as other very important considerations, that remain to explore.

As already mentioned, Gerring and Thacker listed 116 countries ordered according to the degree of Centripetalism. The first thing that catches the eye is that almost all Western European countries are included in the first 25. Actually the first part of the list is dominated by Europe (17 countries out of 25). According to the authors, more Centripetalism corresponds to more good governance. Thus the question arises whether there are some omitted variables that affect the outcome and produces spurious correlations. In fact, at a first glance, it would seem that Centripetalism is correlated with good governance only because it's more likely to find good governance in European states (that for whatever reason – cultural, historical, or other – are more centripetal) than in the rest of the world. In this case, correlation between Centripetalism and good governance may be only coincidental, rather than representing a causal relationship. This may bias the entire analysis, since it is a very strong correlation, involving all the first part of the list. Another consideration is that United States are expected to be the worst governed country in the world, since they are the last in the list (number 116), but this is counter-intuitive and hardly we can state that Turkey, Greece or Botswana (number 17, 20 and 32) are better governed than USA (note that even Switzerland has a very bad position, number 61). Can such important examples be simply ignored? Anyway, Gerring and Thacker applied fourteen specific controls to employ throughout the empirical analysis, included geography, regions (among which there is "Western Countries") and GDP; so even if an high degree of skepticism remains, it seems that their analysis is valuable at least in dealing with statistical correlations.

Nonetheless, what is stunning are the results Gerring and Thacker expressly report. In fact among the three variables, "Parliamentarism shows a particularly strong relationship with good governance, while results for Unitarism are somewhat less consistent. Closed-list PR shows a mixed pattern" [p. 117, 2008]. This interpretation of the results is too much in favour of their theory, as it can be seen in the table below (taken from Gerring and Thacker's book [p. 139]). Only Parliamentarism shows a strong correlation with good governance and clearly it is the one that triggers the positive correlation when the three variables are aggregated forming Centripetalism.

TABLE 6.12. *Summary of empirical tests*

Dependent Variables	Independent Variables			
	Cent	Unit	Parl	Closed-list PR
Political Development				
Tax revenue	+ +	+ +	+ +	+ +
Telephone mainlines	+ +		+ +	– –
Participation	+ +	+ +	+ +	+ +
Democratic volatility	+		+	
Economic Development				
Import duties	+ +	+ +	+ +	
Trade/GDP	+ +	+ +	+ +	+
GDP per capita	+ +		+ +	
Growth volatility			+ +	– –
Human Development				
Infant mortality	+ +	+ +	+ +	
Public health expenditures	+ +		+	+ +
Total schooling	– –	– –	– –	–
Summary				
Good governance (+ or + +)	9/11	5/11	10/11	4/11
Bad governance (– or – –)	1/11	1/11	1/11	3/11

Summary of Centripetalism results based on full models from Tables 6.1–6.11. + + and + indicate statistical significance at the 0.05 and 0.10 levels, respectively, in the expected direction. – – and – indicate statistical significance at the 0.05 and 0.10 levels, respectively, in the unexpected direction. Empty cell indicates that there is no statistically significant relationship.

To underline the positive correlations between Parliamentarism and good governance is like to reinvent the wheel. Lijphart states that there is a strong scholarly consensus in favour of parliamentary government. In the extensive literature on this subject, the relatively few critics have questioned only parts of the pro-parliamentary consensus [p. 81, 2007]. If Gerring and Thacker had discussed any casual mechanism (maybe through case study analysis) about, let's say, any of the few variables linking Unitarism to good governance (for instance why Unitarism produces more tax revenues and more participation, thing that might be plausible) it would have improved the validity of their analysis. But put in this way, results are too faint to give to the theory a real explanatory power. The fact of considering only causal relationship in the long run bring to fanciful, too "generalizable" conclusions. In order to prove the validity of the examined correlations we need to focus to causal mechanisms, thus it is necessary to redefine the unit of analysis to a lower level of aggregation, seeing how one small event triggers another one, better identifying in this way causal relationship (this method concerns more "case study analysis" than "quantitative methods" and is called "process tracing" by George and Bennet [p. 176-178 and p. 207, 2005], or Darren Hawkins [p. 57, 2009]). Even Hellwig asks himself "why is this very short book limited to testing its argument only one way, using time-series cross-section analyses of highly aggregated macro indicators, and not targeted comparative case studies, more disaggregated analyses of a subsample of countries"; he

17

concludes that, as "the authors frequently remind us, the book's goals are modest and the evidence is selective. Conclusions are more suggestive than definitive" [p. 1001, 2009]. Yet, Gerring and Thacker seem to give definitive conclusions. In fact, in discussing the empirical parts of their work, they state that "the preponderance of the evidence rests in favour of centripetal institutions, rather than decentralized ones", and add: "Institutions that pull toward the center, maximizing the twin goals of authority and inclusion in a democratic setting, are on the whole associated with higher levels of political, economic, and human development" [p. 117, 2008]. It's not possible to agree with this last statement. There are no elements at all supporting this conclusion about the connection between good governance and the twin goals of inclusion and authority, unless we consider Parliamentarism an organizational form (or better, the only one) that perfectly embodies the ideals of inclusion and authority. But this has no sense, and it wouldn't have much more sense if considering the combination of Parliamentarism and Unitarism as the organizational forms embodying the ideals of inclusion and authority. Moreover, the last has only a very weak correlation with good governance[9], thus it shouldn't be of

---

[9] This in the empirical findings of Gerring and Thacker, while there is a huge literature both empirical and theoretical underlining the correlation between federalism and good governance. From Tiebout (1956) and Buchanan (1980), to Weingast (2000) and Rodden (2004). Rodden notes that the vast "first generation" theoretical literature about federalism is opposed to an earlier generation of studies underlining the limits of these theories through empirical findings. But he also stresses how "early empirical studies paid little attention to the

help. In conclusion, there is no connection between what is theoretically defined by the two authors as Centripetalism (and their theoretical view is not even shared by all) and good governance.

---

varieties of fiscal and political decentralization" and why "producers of cross-national regressions should be modest about their claims". Now a next generation of empirical studies is approaching, embracing the complexity and diversity of decentralization and considering different orders of causes and effects. Thanks to this, the fit between theory (favouring federalism) and empirical analysis is improving (Rodden, [p. 481-482, 489, 2004]).

References

Bagehot W. (1963), *The English Constitution* (1867), Cornell University Press, New York

George A., Bennet A. (2005), *Case Study and Theory Development in the Social Sciences*, MIT Press, Cambridge (Massachusetts)

Gerring J., Thacker S.C. (2008), *A Centripetal Theory of Democratic Governance*, Cambridge Univeristy Press, Cambridge (UK)

Hawkins D. (2009), *Case Studies* in The SAGE Handbook of Comparative Politics, ed. by Todd Landman and Neil Robinson, Sage publications, London

Hellwig T. (2009), *Book Review: Gerring, J., & Thacker, S. C. (2008). A Centripetal Theory of Democratic Governance* in Comparative Political Studies, Cambridge University Press, Cambridge (UK)

Horowitz D.L. (1985), *Ethnic Groups in Conflict*, University of California Press, Berkeley

Lijpart A. (1999), *Patterns of Democracy: Government Forms and Performance in Thirty-Six Countries*, Yale University Press, New Haven

Lijphart A. (2007), *Thinking about Democracy: Power sharing and majority rule in theory and practice*, Routledge, London

Rodden J. (2004), *Comparative Federalism and Decentralization: On meaning and Measurement*, Comparative Politics 36, 4: 481-500

Tiebout C.M. (1956), *A Pure Theory of Local Expenditures*, Journal of Political Economy, 60: 416-24

Weingast B.R. (2000), *The Comparative Theory of Federalism*, Hoover Institution, Stanford University, Stanford

www.ingramcontent.com/pod-product-compliance
Lightning Source LLC
Chambersburg PA
CBHW050529290526
45786CB00007B/2756